How To Find All Missing Persons / Unsolved Cases. And Collect All Reward Offers. Volume V THE CASE OF DANAE WILLIAMS

David Gomadza

www.twofuture.world

Copyright © 2024 David Gomadza

All rights reserved.

PAPERBACK **ISBN:** 9798325859809

DEDICATION

A better world.

CONTENTS

1   How To Find All Missing Persons / Unsolved Cases And Collect All Rewards Offers . The Formula. Volume V THE CASE OF DANAE WILLIAMS

ACKNOWLEDGMENTS

Tomorrow's World Order

HOW TO FIND ALL MISSING PERSONS / UNSOLVED CASES AND COLLECT ALL REWARD OFFERS THE FORMULA VOLUME V THE CASE OF DANAE WILLIAMS

BACKGROUND INFORMATION

On May 12, 2021, at 8:55 p.m., Danae Williams, age 25, was in her car, stopped at a red light, in the area of NE Martin Luther King, Jr. Boulevard and NE Dekum Street in Portland, Oregon. As the light changed, a silver sedan pulled up along the passenger side of the car and someone fired multiple rounds into the vehicle. Williams was shot and died of her wounds the following day. A passenger in the car was also shot in the head but survived. Investigators believe Williams and her passenger were innocent victims of an ongoing violent dispute between rival gangs.

The #FBI is offering a reward of up to $15,000 for information leading to the arrest and conviction of the individual(s) responsible for the murder of Danae Williams, shot and killed in her car on May 12, 2021, in Portland, Oregon:

TOMORROW'S WORD ORDER'S PRESPECTIVE

This is how we as Tomorrow's World Order solved this case with myself [David Gomadza] as the founder, and the president of the whole world. www.twofuture.world

All information on the website could be write and could be wrong most is totally different from our account in many respect writing my account I did not research anything on the internet so don't be surprised to find out what I am going to say is totally different from all these accounts.

I look at missing persons cases simply based on brain reading that means if I get right person's brain readings then this account is 100% accurate so far.

Signed

David Gomadza

00447719210295

Davidgomadza@hotmail.com

How To Find All Missing Persons / Unsolved Cases. And Collect All Reward Offers. Volume V THE CASE OF DANAE WILLIAMS

Www.twofuture.world

THE FUTURE: THE AFTERLIFE CONVERSATION AND THE COUNCIL OF CREATION

I died God I was shot 3 times at point blank in the head and I died I made calls to the police to come to the rescue but they refused saying I got what I deserved for I used to torment them for being lazy and dump especially Pc artonpqrs who literally shouted one day you gonna need us so bad that you will shit if we don't turn up Now this is a case of revenge for saying stuff that upset others while in a position of weakness now if we look at the facts it seems this woman got what she deserved for she disrespected the law enforcement now what can be of her surely at this point anything can happen to her in a country with so many guns totaling 8.5 billion among the people now what can be said of her after this more likely to be shot now we can see after that a trail of events happening so fast soon she is caught up in a shooting at the market where she survives the gunmen shooting her friend and missing her now imagine offending the police who can arrest anyone and forgive them on grounds that they take her out now what compare this to the fact that she was about to go abroad after the death threats became a problem now Ask this would she had to go the answer is yes to serve her life now what can be of her after this we Ask she could be anything from a sitting duck to the biggest bait ever now let's look at the facts in detail on 28 March 2021 she woke up and said I want to prepare and go to Spain for sometime I think shittitttt is after me I just received a death threat and the message read if you wanna leave don't go you live that means we are so bad you have to go but I think we are so good you will rather stay now if we Ask who sent the message this was a hidden code that beeps inside her sent as code 82345678908901238562l8 it read beep beep beep. Beep beep beep. Beep beep beep beep beep and it was sent by Pc artonspot who had threatened her she instantly ask who the fuck using the same beep saying bee.p beep b.e.e.p and instantly the connection disconnected but left a residue that say hi I am antroprsr and went out of the radar now what can we learn about this case this Pc antrsopsr was a leading police officer who wanted respect among the youths so that they provide for them when their parents die according to him in a road side now this is interesting because this Pc said the same thing and her mother got in an accident but did not die if we are to ask if there was any insolvent the answer is no but... now if we look at this case we can see a lot of things going not as planned but... now let's look at what had happened she had been robbed twice at gun point and was in a recovery position from the last ordeal now if we look at what had happened she had asked people what can be done about these harassment by the law officers now what can be can be if we Ask we can see that she had been in hospital for the treatment of trauma now what can be said about this case it has all the whole marks of harassment and intimidation until day of death that morning the inside text message had rattled her she had failed to cope with the threat but she had some driving to do according to her Now what if we are to ask what can be of her after this then it means that she was destined to die but could have run away now what can be said of her after this she could be dead or for that matter now what could be of her after this then she could be other than now what happened this day will baffle you even though she had not said anything these were were goodbyes to friends and relatives secretly as she was to fly to Spain early in the morning looking forward to a better new life now if we are to ask what can be of anyone after this day life would change for the officers who had gained work because of her now thus is the most bizarre case ever we have looked at in here in the council of creation Now look at what happened until time she was short now can we ignore all the inside calls and arrive at the same conclusion that she was being followed not by gunmen but by hired off duty police officer who in fact shot her for stealing our food and running with it as one puts it now let's look at the facts what happened this day means there was no way she could safely leave her enemies behind they really wanted to take her down and indeed they did beastly saying anyone who solves this case is God or is known to God because there is no human being who will say it as it is exactly because for the first time everything is inside we trained this woman at our own expense today is the day to repay all that back now let's look at this method of inside communication Humans over years have developed sophisticated methods of communicating that will revolutionize the way they talk this method relies on a beep that means who but if with a Fallston at the end it means who you so beep. Is who are you if the reply is beep.beep it means I am him if beep.beep.beep it means I am him who now what is you want to say names of people then what the beep keeps repeating up to 26 times so first beep is a second b third is c so a name like danae would be beepx4 beepx9 beepx1 beepx21 beepx1 and beepx5 now let's look at talking if the beep is bee.p this means how are you today can we talk and if be.ep that means I don't have time next time if b.eep that means I have time but not now so b..eep means we can talk now this is just to find time for the police so they have reason to come in the neighborhood and say hie now let's look why all this is needed police coming unannounced with warrant is classed as harassment in America that lead to dismissal now let's look how they tried to jump this if they come when you have said you have time they are going to roughen you up then ask someone to provide what you want but you pay everything a useless middlemen with literally mouthing to contribute to but with wasted time and emotional damage now this is what is interesting because the police officers themselves need help even with cigarettes they go own to ask shop keepers for cigarettes in return of safeguarding them against theft now let's see what happened this day now let's see the action in play from above the skies in the chamber of creation our highest judge the almighty Yahweh is here now let's Ask a question What can be of an escapee without protection he or she can be a scapegoat and be targeted for destruction now what can be of the police officer they trained her and now fear she would reveal to outsiders how they ask youths for favors that give them constant jobs which is illegal that if proved will lead to dismissal now what can be of her that now she has decided to run away this is the answer she could be killed and die know shat can be of them be dismissed even though it's not a clear cut maybe she won't say anything abroad now this is what happened Pc antrsopsr called three men directly using landlines phones and all were police officers 1 Pc antop 2 Pc rstop and Pc antrpetw who were all of Portuguese origins who kept saying sinuarer sinuarer meaning miss miss in Portuguese as we have discovered through the vast language translations now let's look at what happened this day she looked at what happened to her on this day and cursed so hard she squirted urine in her pants and said what the fuck once she said this somehow [something flew out of the body looking for someone to say the same thing as well that's how what the fuck works] Now Ask what could be of her this day she could be shot and be buried the next day so what could be of them they could simply say what if now Ask what could be of her after this day now we can see clearly that the police officers would not let her go that means she could be killed today because by tomorrow she would be in Spain now let's see what follows she asked them what could be of them and they said zero but... now that rattled her that she got off the car in the middle of the road and puked so hard that she squirted and this time shit herself with fear now let's look what what could be of her after this Now let's look at what can be of her now that she could be murdered now what is and what is not is not clear but if they are zero to match them she could be zero too in most cases means death that is why she shit herself now how can she clean when everyone is beeping after her to get off the road now we can see her confused of what to do can she cleanup or jump in the car she jumped into the car and screamed before Pc artop opened fire saying bitch get out of the car I want this ride or God is going to judge you before sending you to hell to wait and die forever because people who play with the police in this country must end up dead because your acts makes others resent us so I signed your death certificate die and I will walk free because you shit yourself who shits himself before death never God expect clean people and predefined system prohibits shitting before death but after death now you challenged God how can he even see you when you die I tell you straight you die you go to court I don't know and they decide how you died so you go to the right place you say I die then God say okay what did you do then you say I was killed after shitting myself and God will say go to hell and rest for a while until judgement day I am telling you this so you remember me in afterlife I can send you straight away to him if I blast you again in the head then you must say I got blasted twice then died now God will look at you and say what did you do then he will say okay go to afterlife and wait now if we all blast you at the same time then if you go to court God will simply say that was a violent deaths and you must go to hell now this is critical these men are telling her how this court functions and they have never been dead or here how? Now if we Ask what can this court as an answer to all three cases I guess he is right humans have learnt to judge others as well using our predefined manuals inside human heads code

88998765432101892840986354178099 now what can be of humans in sight of God God works in miracle our ways but is not as predictable as humans thought but in this case Pc artop is right God would pass these three judgement now what can we say about this artop as a police officer he was okay until when his own son was shot in the head and died in his arms that when he started searching about God to find out what happened to his son over the years he had become so fearless that he walked in front of men raising their guns and said no one will kill me today because but...now you can see that he had learnt the art of manipulation very well that day he had sent code 896658678982108677187098208 to everyone repeatedly until everyone had a code and shouted you can't kill me today because you can't but... now this stance was to win him his favors with the rest of the group that he can free people's brains and let them decide not to shoot now what can be of him this day he was destined to kill and kill he did despite all others saying it was just to roughen her up so that she can't sell us abroad now what could be of this police officer he could be dead in jail because someone is proven to prove he can't control him now this is what happened she screamed and covered her face fearing for what they call a face off where she is shot to literally remove the face so that God does not instantly recognize her now what would be the effect of this she would have been sent to hell instead because three men shooting one will traumatized the brain that to recover she would need to sleep for a long time and then do to afterlife but only in hell are people allowed to sleep in heaven there is no sleeping because if you sleep in heaven you lose something called asyopqrstuvwxyz this thing makes you fly at night if you need to visiting other galaxies so every traumatized person as a general rule must be sent to hell just for sleeping but nothing to do with the devil the devil knows God send his own people but as patience to hell as per their agreement dated 20 June
000000000000000000000000000000000000000000000000
000000000000000000000000000000000000000000000000
000000000000000000000000000000000000000000000000
000000000000000000000000000000000000000000000000
000000000000000000000000000028698367890286778901832106

654832102864810998310
Now having said this you should ask what can be of humans they can only be another who might want to be Yahweh this artop is just arrogant but I can fix him said Yahweh looking upset okay he can read my brain but that's all humans can do would he put me in this poor girls shoes I don't know much about humans if he want he can be me but how long can he last his acts jeopardize my safety now I know now it's him trying to hack me why not ask me there is one image of me on earth that he can have and literally be me and I will offer him all the gold and silver and no one will object or they all die if ghey do now if we Ask what can be of him now Yahweh [be merciful to humans] can actually grant him his image as there is one on earth on a first find first claim now if we are to look at what could be of humans then this is the answer Yahweh can increase power and wealth among humans and can show mercy instead of killing this artop he can actual give him the only of his images on earth which one must find to be Yahweh not just that but with the riches of the world I tell you the person who finds this image is the richest powerful and smartest of all for 25 billion years now lets see what can be and would be of humans humans can be near to God if one finds his image that means humans can be in the council of creation for the first time in 89689738410998877662849810 billion years now if we Ask what can be of this artop who has gone to lengths to study the highest judge he could be put in the highest judges shoes to decide cases and make judgements or can have his pain sockets removed first for imitating Yahweh without authorisation now let's see what can be done and what could be of humans without Yahweh humans will be lost and Yahweh will be the almighty king forever and ever now what can be of humans without artop artop is a crook according to our records but we must give him credit too for before the loss of his son he was loyal and just wanted to finish work and go to his son Aserpetros who from time to time would call and say hey just checking you haven't forgotten about me your favorite son now this day he woke up early in the morning and said I could be with you today but... and stopped now what this does is to find a solution that can make him feel better his asm said do you want a remorse justification that will sooth you internally without even getting caught forever because I

will double you clone you and send you two different places at the same time and do everything in everyone's eyes just like God does to others who he loves but are in hell he looked confused and said can you clone my son and asm said son is dead I can't because when you die all cloning properties dies too so cloning is hard but you are alive with all cloning properties that means you can clone yourself and both go each way then split only st the time of the ...you know blah blah blah and instantly he asked you said God can clone people in hell he wants?
Did he clone my son?
Has he cloned my son?
[ ] Instantly asm said yes God loves your son for there is no other son on earth who has shown love for his father his creator like you now if we are to ask what can be of him God had already cloned his son now we can start to understand why he started knowing too much about God his son would visit him the cloned one at night and talk to him in his sleep telling him exactly what happened on day of death this is his story I was walking down ghe street and a car stopped in front of me and a man said your father killed my brother two days ago but...and pulled his gun and blasted him one short in the head and drove off if we are to ask who this person was this is the answer he was petrosve artendedss who asked for a transfer to another city and days before he leaves his brother is ambushed by the police in what was described as a botched robbery now if we look deeper into this case we can see that this was a targeted attack the police to stop him going after training their beep technique were unwilling to risk it so decided to target his brother as a robber so that whatever he says would easily be refuted as they are all a crooked family now what could have been of this family after the deaths people would look at them as if there was no other things they wanted from there now what can be of them and the future blink as the police would do everything to deny this and even get them attacked now what can be of this family they could be attacked again in the future now let's look what happened to her afterwards in detail now this Pc artop is in front of her with a gun judging her to see if she skips the court and go straight to hell now if we Ask what can be of artop now with his arrogance he could be still at large with nothing against him now let's look at why he was

so arrogant no human being can solve this case now artop was now the chief superintended of the force seeing complicated cases because of his ability to solve comes cases satisfactory beyond reasonably doubt and the answer was that through the generosity of his Majesty artop somehow could read judgements of all cases and reproduce them for profit but the force refused to offer him reward money which had given him hope of wealth now that was gone he used this gratitude to challenge the creator in a battle of wits he started imitating Yahweh through his son he would ask his son what is Yahweh to him and say Yahweh is a selfish God who gave up his son Jesus to save the world when he could simply has cloned all before they died and save all the same process now if we look at this can this be true? Yahweh is childless he doesn't need kids because he can create rather than produce produce is for lower level beings now if we Ask why artop was obsessed with Yahweh his accusation was that God had felt jealous about the dedication of his son and wanted him for himself and had actually cloned him and took him this is proof that he had God him killed for himself as such he must kill this God now let's look at the events leading to his son's death he had been part of this targeting to remove possibilities of people reporting them outside now let's look closely what can be of artop he can be the boss and dictates the pace and course of things now let's see what can be of the girl she could be the pace maker but according to artop now if we are to ask what is to be of artop he could be the best cope ever for he had excess to all cases all 2486 missing people cases could be solved earning his men huge bonuses enough to get free company cars per case that becomes yours after only 5 years per case meaning you solve twenty cases then you have twenty cars after 5 years but artop had limited access to God his son only came at night but in his sleep and tell me about the case he was working on but artop wanted to read all cases alive and had discovered that this was possible but Yahweh has to give you authorisation that way you can publish them and use then to solve all cases if this was so that would have meant all his men multi millioners something he had already promised when he first met his cloned son now God had removed authorisation by declining his so when he heard of the accusations that he nearly used his other son for eletetetetetetetetetetetetetetetetetetetetey the greatest punishment everywhere pain sockets are removed and eletate is removed for vocabulary now let's see what could be of artop without his cloned son now he could not solve anything but could only infer things most of which turned out to be very wrong now he became really about everything to cover for his ignorance when a case is brought out his men would say it's solved already but ended up getting everything wrong this is because at the beginning he would not even look at the facts but would wrote from his head without anything but after everything stopped he tried writing using notes but his men started taunting him that he list his ability because his ghost son had been sent to hell for refusing that there was a God by challenging God what happened is that he said God don't exist because my son died as such he would fight anyone who said otherwise now let's look at the facts he had lost a child and was traumatic and wanted to be a father again to his own child but he had been given that chance but without knowing accusing him of wanting his son and got him killed but a counter from the highest judge was that he had deliberately had this son so that he sent it to me as a link to the files but I am not sure how as he had learnt to hide his thoughts from me by using a code 39867891028677861098738 that would divert all this thoughts back to himself and ask it to replay everything so that his memory becomes the richest in the world even more than God's now if we look at all this he had written notes a lot on how to talk to God in times of trouble but all those methods were meant for humans gods uses different syntaxes without constants as such all his messages were gibberish I tried several translators and they all failed to decipher his messages but it only came clear when I cloned his son that he spoke of me more than often but in an arrogant what if manner just to provoke my response without substance now let's look at the facts artop was advanced but lacked love for me he only wanted fame and pleasing his men who he had promised millions of dollars in solved cases meaning just earthly things with no ambition of ruling the earth which is not one of the conditions of being Yahweh now let's look at what can be of artop without ambition to rule the world Yahweh would only give his image to someone with ambition to rule all earth by himself and ideal 3 others in stand by now let's look at what this could be without

Yahweh nothing really now if I am to ask what can be of artop with a little bit of Yahweh he could rule the world now what can be of artop on his own without his men would be like him and his son peaceful now what can be of Yahweh without artops son the same Yahweh need no son and what can be of artop's son without Yahweh lost and in hell now what could be of heaven without artop or his son he never died but when he does its up to Yahweh to decide which is right but we can say that there has been some issues with non payment of reward money this is because the company refused to award him because this was part of his job so coming and claiming when he worked for them had raised controversy to such an extent they had hired lawyers because admitting would mean huge loses in tunes of millions as they had to pay huge bonuses the reasons why the bonuses were so high was the difficult level this case had been given a difficult level of 90 out of 100 meaning impossible to Crack now artop without the ability to read and after losing his son wanted a way out dead or alive but what can be of him without a police job he could start again and start claiming when he leave making him rich but there was a catch he did not read the small print because Rewards are payments to people who created the job the murder if you like now can we as what can be of him out of the force he can be a good person who fear Yahweh now what can we say of him as a person and a father who lost a child a good man now let's everything in action now that you have seen all possibilities of what could be as required by the council of creation Now what is to be of danae williams after this day she could be anything but she was destined to die but she could still escape but the man playing God had other selfish plans now we can reveal why he did it now his real motive all this about case he wanted God to talk to him directly so that he can download all cases unto a hard drive and sell to the highest bidder but he wanted to show the world power that God exist and one day he will be able to read all cases one by one and write reports for each case then use these to get rewards in the end and if we Ask Yahweh thinks about this first Yahweh questioned his intention why and motive even though these seem the same at times they are different now let's first check what's permitted and is not the cases are a guideline to what happens when a person dies that the first stop is the court of creation for his case to be decided on preliminary grounds then be see what can be done to lessen the pain now let's check what could be of this artop he could indeed download all 85 billion cases and sell them valuable but then again then what at some point his money would run dry now let's see what is allowed and not allowed first to authorized people they need only work on a case at a time hence download all is not permitted because of privacy as there is nothing more private than thier deaths secondly selling with the hope of a profit is partly denied solve the case then collect the reward but mentioning of the need to collect and a collection method is okay but selling to highest bidder is denied now let's see what is authorized to unauthorized people selling of cases is not authorized and can result in premature deaths if not careful selling downloads of all cases no matter what is not authorized now let's see what could be of Yahweh if artop is to win the battle of wits artop here is going to read rights of his victim and decide for her where she can go jumping the council of creation then asking not to be named in the records so that it shows someone else called unknown doing the same job so that according to him is a direct challenge on his authority but to us this means nothing we can decide cases without his majestic ruler Yahweh now let's look at what can be of Yahweh after the challenge yes surely if the angels follow this this command threatens that the person is allowed and can replace Yahweh but then again given the circumstances it means that Yahweh would have now to find a way of authorizing artop just for that case and remove his pain sockets and take his eletetetetetetetetetetetetereteteteteteteteteteteteteteteteey now what can be said of Yahweh after this the only ruler in the world what artop was doing was showing Yahweh loop holes people can imitate him and this is his grave mistake helping people know how to imitate Yahweh is punishable by death now let's see what can be of artop without Yahweh,'s mercy he would be lost without the all mighty now let's look back at what happened to the girl in real time then analyze artop's motives now faced with a gun she looked lost and said don't shoot I shit myself God will automatically send me to hell he looked confused how smart she was he had not anticipated that then she said if you shoot I will ask God to swap our places mine for yours if it fits so HD stopped and thought about it and aimed and lastly she said shoot me all of you so that I automatically go to hell and rest with this shit I risk being put in hell fire for eternity but... instantly all three raised their guns and aimed hard then she said if I die instantly say go and rest in hell so that I skip the council of creation if they know I shit myself before death they won't look at my case because shit and the council is against predefined rules so she closed her eyes and prayed father forgive them for they don't know what they do this is the opposite of what he wanted if he don't know what he is doing how can he be challenging God to a game of wits so he said harshly all you stop I don't want to get you all involved it's between me and the girl so you all leave I will shot her by my self and if they refuse I will run and leave them to kill you she refused because one person 3 shots is not violent enough to be classed as violent in the council of creation but instead the others ran away living him with her Now what followed yes is a show of power to Yahweh but in vain if I Ask why this is the answer he quickly triggered a number 8698762832489778677890r8412 that can easily change the send to back to that person then as that happened she said lord if I sinned forgive me but if not then change my place for his in hell I don't mind I rather be asleep than dine with you when you get us killed easily why you never showed when people need you? I die happy these r.e.beep are a real problem to youths you should keep killing them like you used to those days I am ready artops raised the gun and said now I will show you that there is no God then he raised his hand and said I want to kill you so violently that me alone will send you to hell now that you know that there is no God he pulled three guns from his paints self attached together but all with one trigger and said is this violent enough 3 in 1 and you are gone now what can be of evil men and God one day he judge them all harshly with no mercy now let's see what happened artop to invoke the wrath of God must shoot all at once so that it classed as a violent crime scene now alone it can and will never but alone with modified guns he can create the most violent crime ever now all he had to do was to blast her so fast and hard that instead of three single ones he will blast her 9 times in less than a second repeating exact same place so that there is no bullet match all sizes will vary and everything will not fit that means on earth no one will ever solve this crime for only God will know the truth now let's look at what happened exactly as if playing everything in repeat slow motion according to the translation now let's Ask what can be of danae williams from now totally dead this man will not stop for he wants to prove a case to God that he can also be powerful one day now what can be of him and God God can easily ask him what if and start the end of him with long start now let's see exactly what happened she tried to ran soon after realizing that death was near but now she remember about the shit then she asked others what can be of her then no one answered others here means God means others other wise it makes no sense as per translation now can we ask what can be of him then this is the answer he can wake up dead but he is clever when it matters he diverted everything back to her and after her send.ya calls he diverted back to God now this is one of the direct challenges that make everything make sense about him he wanted Yahweh not to get the messages of all victims and saves these in a file which he can use after living work but how can when he can find Yahweh do he devices a plan he let the person call for help and to keep Yahweh on the line enough to download everything he needed while is answering the call then use the recording to prove Yahweh and be respected all over the world as the greatest or the most smart one they say who he finds Yahweh,'s image becomes the greatest in the world for the world's wealth is his and he has keys to live forever here on earth now can we ask what could be of this person he would literally command any creature on earth by simple commands like ask.ya.now if that happens all humans shall accept him instantly as their leader [ask.ya.davidgomadza.ya.now] Now if we Ask what can be of her then death now was imminent there was no other way now if we Ask what can be then this is the answer she can go to hell straight because 9 bullets would render her traumatized forever now what if he could forgive her and forget about the ordeal what would then happen this is because what can be is What could be that means she could die easily and go on to hell where she now wanted now looking at artop he deliberately planned everything so that she would refuse heaven for fear of instant rejection now she opened her mouth as the first three hit her unexpected and so brutal she squirts with orgasm and laughed as a cushiony effect and he said I sense an orgasm now if we look clearly no one can have orgasm if traumatized now if we check source of orgasm then we can see that it's artop's code 82983867845382109848687828019867851 2366 that could have triggered the artificial orgasm as it is the only artificial orgasm that was recorded [oh my God I thought he was going to leave me alone if he knew I was not afraid to die instant an inside message by some animal that never works that is on her right shoulder waking up for the first time said danger of death escape to heaven the classification said not trauma detected but an orgasm she looked at him once and said if I had the chance but...that eager him enough to blast her again this time cursing that stopped the second artificial orgasm code scheduled to come after this Now with everything stopped the first artificial orgasm had created 10 squawks that they had initiated about to explode that she squirted again heavily with the third set of bullets and he said yeah babe and quickly stood there hiding everything and changing clothes into a police uniform but one person find it odd that if you hear gunshots you would go to the car and wear police uniform but he said if I got shot the people will know that the fugitive was still out there now let's look at her death in detail after multiple orgasms that lasted after death as the squanks accelerated as she died all calls for help were disabled by the orgasms as this is not part of the predefined procedure and no call for help was sent and honestly Yahweh did not receive snatching about her to his shook that he tried to reach for artop from heaven but somehow received a message that said one step ahead of you imagine if I can catch you instead down to earth but...I want to be your representative on earth and inherit all the wealth there was a beep at the end that lodged inside Yahweh he looked lost and said what can be done about this arrogant sutrsstursssturdeferdetssadtuvwxyz meaning arrogant evil bastard that can never represent me ever how can hiding calls for help be a challenge of wits? But... now let's look at this incident in detail artop to him to prove his wits had to deny Yahweh access to people's messages sent using send.ya now if we look deeper we can see that he used code 897i684838287869542108910 to divert any messages sent to send.ya back to that person this means he can have time to get his gadget he named the God's advocate to record everything that happens at that time and send to his lab to be analyzed all this to prove that he can talk to God according to him he can say for sure what is needed of him and actually threatened to pull him down instead okay that alarmed Yahweh once and he said better try I think you have suffered huge trauma as such you go to hell Yahweh stretched his hand to suck his soul from earth while alive hoping to send the 8287866543210891089483621O to retrieve all humans without souls by getting them killed instantly whatever means possible but artop instantly activated code 186848689014687009838672468984100 and said by whose authority because the council of creation said no one shall be taken before their time as such I refuse and there is nothing you can do to me but... he instantly activated code 9867824867982867718492687718S and said can we talk one on one I can hear you listen I made a mistake I thought this is what you do in whatif but he looked a bit suspicious and said okay let's talk whilst we can then suddenly he grabbed Yahweh but the collar of one of his friends to lift him but realised that something was not rights now this is page interesting thing as he tried to lift Yahweh something jumped out of his body saying is that Yahweh I better run before he turns me into eletatetetetetetetetetetetetetetetetetetetereteteteteteteteteteteteterey now let's look what is the punishment of attacking Yahweh it is dead by being drained alive the most painful of all because to get to the eletate he must have all pain sockets removed that means maximum pain for each action now let's look what followed he said I can send you to hell by a simple code. [ ] Now what can be of Yahweh at this moment in time now what happened is that if it was Yahweh alone this human might have send Yahweh to hell as for sure fir the first time in the history of mankind now as Yahweh struggled with this human we intervened and stopped this by a simply phrase humans o humans and gods to gods then everything stopped he quickly grabbed his soul and said eletetatetetetetetetetetetetetetetetetetetetetetetetetetetetetetet etetetetetetetetetetetetetetetetetetetetetetetetetetetetetetetetet etetetetetetetetetetetetetetetetetetetetey but as he took time to increase the pain decibels artop activate another code [ ] and said [ ] then said what can be of [ ] then asked if anyone lost a child and if a thief cloned him for himself then used eletete to kill him back I want to know because I am a giving father and must receive answers but now he said I can leave you if you clone my son again but Yahweh said you are forever human these tricks can only get your soul killed forever and I mean it don't think you can provoke us and win instantly something cried Yahweh have mercy on humans looking at this we can see that this artop had planned everything way ahead of the challenge the message came from the creature that forever sleeps on the right shoulder of humans just to warn of final danger now what can be of humans if they challenge Yahweh that creature only spoke once but everything else in everyone said the same thing like a chorus and Yahweh stopped and said I forgive him but forever help no one has attempted to send the ruler to hell for a son as such you will lose another son son until you have nothing he expected an apology instead Yahweh got angry and slashed at him that instantly killed his soul and now inside him that creature said run for Yahweh will send the xxrstuvwxyzttrstuvwxyz to collect all humans removed of their souls by Yahweh or his authorisation he looked confused as there were no changes he expected to slump and die but a message from that creature said you can't ever go to heaven anymore for your soul has been removed but hell is still an option he smiled and said I nearly sent the mighty ruler to hell I must be the greatest of all never his representative for a fraction when you can have it all I will try again now he switched off his gadget he was using and cried so hard that he nearly sent God to hell but what would be the effect of this sending youth understand that God send his own people to hell to sleep to recover from trauma the more you sleep the better things become now I know his aim was not to kill Yahweh but to send him for getting his son killed but this is a lie because he had sex with a prostitute without condom and said we will simply get rid of what comes that means he wanted a baby he can later kill then use that baby as a link to Yahweh and solve all cases making him the greatest that ever lived meaning riches for each case now what we have learnt is that when Yahweh was reciting the eletete he was using that to download all cases in Yahweh's body [] Now what can be of this case Yahweh simply said all stolen cases must be returned to their respective owner and instantly all returned he then said who ever stole once should not be allowed to steal again otherwise its a breach of security punishable by eletete so he laughed and somehow he realised the funny part of that after he then said today a human has outsmarted the all mighty and he has earned only grief from me even if he wanted to be my representative how can I look others in the eyes around him I sent a message to the devil to deny even his son instantly someone where should I go and Yahweh said eletatetetetetetetetetetetetetetetetetetetetetetetetetetetetet etetetetetetetetetetetetetetetetetetetetetetetetetetetetetetet etetetetetetete...and then y the creatures on human shoulders ran out in panic without a word and said say daddy take for getting me killed if not now when you come okay he smiled everyone sweated hard and all said Yahweh the just and merciful now when the police arrived she was sending last calls for help saying I died God please accept me it does not matter I want to be in heaven than asleep and God said what happened you are not in my system of recognizing people she said he diverted back to me and Yahweh raised his hand and the message played in people mouths oh God help me the cop is bad news he wants to send me to you prevent this then I know and everyone else that you are the greatest greater than this shittitttt instantly a beep went off and orgasm senses caught all and as far as the council know Yahweh never had sex despite having a wife Catitighit who has sex organs that means for billions he never felt what it is to orgasm because he asked why she struggling to breath with her vagina with a faint arousal his screamed with panic first confused and listened only to experience what orgasm is like she cried and said be merciful on humans my greatest he looked confused and said I am this is the human way of life not for the gods she cried secretly feeling exactly what she felt and said what human does this to gods before she squirts but Yahweh said lock detachment it's meant to separate us instead everyone locked in and the locking in dockets extended and the all locked in all of them above 20 and for sure he heard someone on the lock to his right side now this sets the commotion because Yahweh stood up and said I will fix you but he started receiving messages of all people who had died using code [ ] Now the effect was to trigger self help mechanism instead of helping others and instantly he said coward saving his own arse when there is a call for help I go and help others a real god

But he had cheated by flooding Yahweh's gates with messages so that when full what can he do other than self preserve what he did he discovered that humans have found a way to divert the send.ya messages to databases and he got really furious and said any human who reverse this is forever indebted to me for these messages extend the gods lives by billion of years now what can be of Yahweh at this point in time Yahweh can be who he is a mighty ruler and a just judge now let's conclude the case danae Williams was blasted 9 times with 3 guns artificially joined together at an angle of 33 degrees the Trajectory of death and her brain went blank on seeing this angle and as the squirt code arrive it made her squirt first and then panicked as she recall the ordeal now life was taken only message to Yahweh was I got killed and died by artops with his accomplice three guns who does this this is violent as such I demand to go to hell Yahweh help.
The end

THE CLAIM

The Reward Offer

THE COLLECTION

www.twofuture.world/donate

ABOUT DAVID GOMADZA

Visit www.twofuture.world

Signed David Gomadza
Ask.davidgomadzaauthorised.licensed.checkya.askya.ya
14may2.27pm
Scotland
00447719210295
Davidgomadza@hotmail.com
Info@twofuture.world
www.twofuture.world

www.ingramcontent.com/pod-product-compliance
Lightning Source LLC
Chambersburg PA
CBHW031516210526
45464CB00007B/2943